I Believe

Juan D. Bautista

I BELIEVE

iUniverse books may be ordered through booksellers or by contacting:

iUniverse LLC
1663 Liberty Drive
Bloomington, IN 47403
www.iuniverse.com
1-800-Authors (1-800-288-4677)

ISBN: 978-1-4917-3961-7 (sc)
ISBN: 978-1-4917-3960-0 (e)

Library of Congress Control Number: 2014912038

Printed in the United States of America.

iUniverse rev. date: 07/09/2014

I want to dedicate this book to all those who struggle with their faith on a daily basis. My prayer is that these stories may help others to trust Jesus more every day.

This book is also dedicated to my beautiful wife, Angie, who has stood by me for the last fourteen years, and to my children: J. M., Gladisel, and Anabella.

My everlasting thanks go to my dear friend J. D. Blanco, to all the team members at iUniverse, and to all those who have prayed for my family and me.

I wish people to stop running church as if it were a business
And that we would be filled with Christ's love and forgiveness.
I wish pulpits to be filled with the Spirit of God
And not the latest Hollywood mod.

I wish preachers would preach like my Lord Jesus did,
Not by words or by arrogance, but by mercy and good deeds.
I wish that one day, when God comes, He would find on this world
A people, a church whose Christ Jesus is Lord.

I wish people could focus on God's glory and praise,
Not on things that divide us, such as money and race.
If at any moment we see our neighbors in need,
Think what Jesus would do, not what Satan just did.

I wish Christians would focus on the heavenly mansions
And be filled with His presence and His tender compassion.
And on that day when His glory dwells on this earth,
We will all be made new and free through His name

Contents

Preface

Today the world appears to be running further and further from God. People seem to have outgrown their belief in God as though He was some mythical concoction like Santa Claus or a superhero from a comic book.

I Believe is my personal testimony and an account of the life lessons I've learned. I have shared my dreamed revelations, answered prayers, blessings granted by strangers, and even my encounters with God Himself. I hope my spiritual journey will help strengthen your faith in Christ and remind you of the imminent, chaotic end of this world as we know it. These stories are a constant reminder that Jesus will return very soon to take His followers to live with Him in the heavenly courts.

Currently, it is very common to hear people talk about their wonderful experiences in which God has helped them in different situations. The truth of the matter is that God can work in mysterious and supernatural ways, and He manifests Himself to people by various means.

Unfortunately, there are many individuals who only pretend to have an encounter with Christ, which causes skepticism when genuine Christians recount their own stories. By no means do I intend to criticize or point a finger at those who have misrepresented God's power or have falsely claimed to witness it. However, I want to show the world that my God is not only all-powerful but that He is a living God who is willing to use His power on behalf of His children.

Like a great majority of people, I did not have the privilege of being born into circumstances where the gospel was known, but at nineteen years of age, I had the most wonderful encounter with Jesus. It was one of the greatest moments that I have ever experienced in my life.

Since that time, I have witnessed many extraordinary occurrences in my life and in the lives of my loved ones, one of which was the Lord's gift of a wonderful family—and an even more wonderful wife, who compliments my faith. Over the years in my spiritual journey, I have held steadfast to God's Word, and I have seen that, indeed, "I can do all things through Christ who strengthens me" (Philippians 4:13 NKJV).

This is why I believe!

1

God Provides

Bread from Heaven

"I am the living bread that came down from heaven. Whoever eats this bread will live forever. This bread is my flesh, which I will give for the life of the world" (John 6:51 NIV).

Abram is considered the father of faith. The Bible says this when talking about him: "Abram believed the LORD, and he credited it to him as righteousness" (Genesis 15:6 NIV).

There are many blessings for those who believe God and depend on His mercy the way Abram did. We should take into consideration that if God provides food for the wild animals and clothes the wildflowers, He will also provide for us.

On one occasion, after waking up and looking at my alarm clock, I realized that I had overslept by forty-five minutes. I quickly began to rush through my daily routine so I could leave home as soon as possible and make it to work on time. Finally, I got into my car and began my journey to work.

While I drove, I listened to the *Bible Experience* CDs I'd purchased previously. On that particular day, I was listening to the book of Matthew—one of my favorites— and I heard the beautiful way that Jesus taught us to pray to the Father and communicate with Him. Immediately I lowered the volume and started to pray and praise my God and Father.

I decided to stop at a gas station to buy a hot chocolate, and only when I got to the cash register did I realize that my wallet was missing. Then I remembered that I had put it on the counter inside my garage at home. Embarrassed, I left the hot chocolate on the counter, returned to my car, and continued my drive to work. I felt somewhat worried, as I was not sure what I would do without my wallet. How was I going to eat on this day? I began to pray, asking God to "give me this day my daily bread."

When I arrived at work, I parked my car behind the store and walked to the front, where my eyes beheld an astonishing sight. In a shopping cart standing right outside the front door was a long bag full of bread. Could the Lord have been more literal or acted more quickly? I just had to chuckle. As I took the bread, I praised the one who had made the heavens and earth, thanking Him for being my God and my provider and for teaching me why I should depend on Him.

It is my prayer that we would all feel the way I do as I describe this story. My heart is full of gladness and joy to know that God loves us so much. It may be that we have bigger problems than not having lunch for the day. It may be that our home or car is about to be repossessed—or something even worse. But today, let us depend on God to provide, since He is the owner of all the gold and resources of the universe.

"Surely God is my help; the Lord is the one who sustains me" (Psalm 54:4 NIV).

God of the Impossible

"Ask and it will be given to you; seek and you will find; knock and the door will be opened to you. For everyone who asks receives; the one who seeks finds; and to the one who knocks, the door will be opened" (Matthew 7:7–8 NIV).

When we study the Old Testament, we can easily see that the most notable men in biblical history are those men whose trust and foundation was placed upon God. Men, such as Enoch, Elijah, Moses, and David were men of faith and prayer and total dependence on God.

In 2008, the economy in the United States began to deteriorate, which forced me to venture into other states in search of work. I remember one day in April when my wife Angie informed me that she needed to make a few payments to bring her accounts up to date. The amount was relatively small, but at that particular moment, I was

$160 short of the total amount needed. I decided to go for a drive so I could think and ask God to enlighten me and to supply our current need.

I drove around in circles on the streets of the Bronx for approximately an hour before deciding to head back home. As I drove homeward, I prayed once more, asking God to provide according to His riches. I came to a stop at a red light at an intersection, and as pedestrians crossed in front of my vehicle, I noticed that there were several twenty-dollar bills on the street. I could not believe my eyes. No one else seemed to see the money. They stepped on the bills, but they did not bend down to pick them up, as though perhaps it was beneath their social status to do so. Since no one was picking up the money, I got out of my car and gathered up the bills in the street. Upon returning to my car and counting the amount, I began to cry. I held in my hands exactly $160.

I do not know if anyone can feel what I felt at that moment. It was something so incredible for a person to experience. I acknowledged then that there is nothing impossible for God and that if I made of Him the center of my life, He would also bless me as He had blessed Daniel and King David on so many occasions recorded in the Bible. I do not mean that we should serve God simply so that He will supply our needs. Rather, we should serve God out of love and our own willingness. And out of His love for us, God will supply all our needs according to all His riches in glory in Christ Jesus!

Grace Overflowing

"God is my helper! The Lord is the provider for my life" (Psalm 54:4 GWT).

Not too long ago, Angie and I surveyed the wicked corruption that abounds in New York City, and we began to look for a quieter area where we could raise our children. Although our finances were somewhat limited, we decided to keep on searching anyway, looking for a house on the outskirts of the city.

After a year, some friends told us about a town in Connecticut where we might find what we were searching for. We scouted the town and were happy with the tranquility and lifestyle there. I had always desired a house that would be safe for my children with a backyard where the kids could play and run. More importantly, I wanted a wooded area where I could retreat in prayer with my heavenly Father. A month or two later, we beheld the house where we wanted to live.

Upon finding such a house, we readily made an offer to the seller, which, to our surprise, was accepted. Throughout the entire process, Angie and I were dreading the day when the deal would close, as we did not have even one-fourth of the amount needed to buy the house. Two days before the closing, Angie prayed and asked God not to let us go empty-handed and be shamed. We still needed $9,000.

That same night, Angie had a dream in which she was at the register of a grocery store. She was ready to pay for some items when she noticed that she was short on the total amount needed. Reluctantly, she handed over the two bills in her hand and waited for the cashier to say that she was short on the amount. To her surprise, the cashier handed back the money along with an extra portion. Angie told the cashier that she had made a mistake, but the cashier replied, "No, everything is just fine." When Angie woke up, she told me her dream, and right then we knew that God had made provision for our need.

When the day of the closing came around, Angie and I showed up with all the money we had, which was $7,500. At the time of the closing, the bank representative decided that the bank would cover the majority of the costs that we had been meant to cover, and so did the seller. By the time the closing concluded, we left with $2,500 dollars cash in our hands and new appliances for our kitchen.

God certainly is amazing and good! He is merciful, supplying all of our needs when we trust him. He is our present help in times of trouble. If we would only believe, we would see great and extraordinary things happen in our daily lives.

"Don't be afraid, for I am with you. Don't be discouraged, for I am your God. I will strengthen you and help you. I will hold you up with my victorious right hand" (Isaiah 41:10 NLT).

God Will Provide

"And this same God who takes care of me will supply all your needs from his glorious riches, which have been given to us in Christ Jesus" (Philippians 4:19 NLT).

In 2002 my first child was born. Angie and I decided to name him Juan Marcos (John Mark) in honor of the New Testament author of the gospel of Mark. Juan Marcos's arrival gave me a complete sense of joy and happiness, and his presence has taught me to depend on my heavenly Father in all life's situations.

One Saturday afternoon after the church service, Angie and I wanted to visit her mother, who happened to live nearby. We failed to notice that we had forgotten to pack any diapers for the baby, who was only a few months old at the time. Of course, Juan Marcos acted within the laws of nature and relieved himself in his diaper.

Now he was in need of a diaper change, but we had none. Angie and I did not want to break the Sabbath by going to the store to buy a bag of diapers, so we were a bit distressed. We also did not want to drive home with the baby and risk any incidents in the car. In my distress, I grabbed my mother-in-law's apartment keys and stepped out to take a walk and have a talk with God.

When I stepped out of the elevator, I felt a strong urge to open my mother-in-law's mailbox and retrieve her mail. I followed my intuition and opened the mailbox—and could not believe my eyes. It was impossible to conceive just how much love God had for a being as insignificant as me. There was a promotional package from a nearby store, addressed to Angie, containing a single diaper in the exact size my son wore. I quickly made my way back upstairs to the apartment to share this wonderful experience of God's love with Angie and my mother-in-law. They were amazed at what I told them.

I'm sure that a lot of us out there would chalk this experience up to mere luck and coincidence, but for me, this was proof that God truly watches out for my every need. It reminded me of the words in a well-known hymn: "If His eye is on the sparrow, then I know He watches me." Since my experience that day, I know in my heart and believe that there is no need outside the reach of my God.

There are so many wonderful promises in the Word of God for all of us. It is His desire that we come to trust Him and depend on Him. I understand that it may be easier said than done when it comes to faith, but Matthew 17:27 states, "For truly, I say to you, if you have faith like a grain of mustard seed, you will say to this mountain, 'Move from here to there,' and it will move, and nothing will be impossible for you."

Let us remember that we can do all things through Christ, who gives us strength, and that when we ask, believing, God will grant us our petitions.

2

Keeping Your Promises

Call from Above

As I have said before, "Today, if you hear his voice, do not harden your hearts as you did in the rebellion" (Hebrews 3:15 NIV).

Music has been a very important and influential force in my family, and many of my family members are professional musicians. I grew up loving and embracing the wonderful music of the Dominican Republic, but when I met the Lord, I promised to sing for His glory and honor and only for Him.

In 2008 while I was a teacher at a Christian school in New York City, I felt the need to experience something different, to make a change in my life. I felt an urge, a longing within me, to do as the Prodigal Son had done and experience the world for myself. I decided I wanted to venture into the music world, singing in the Latin genre of bachata.

I first talked it over with Luis Manuel, my brother in Christ, who advised me to think it over very carefully. He said that he would support my decision, whichever way I decided to go. Three months later, I found myself in a recording studio, finishing an array of songs for my CD album and promotional tour.

So began my journey into the music industry, a career that, it seemed, would skyrocket immediately. Close friends, family, and other church members advised me to leave that type of life behind and return to the correct path. They reminded me of my promise to sing for God's glory and honor, but it was difficult for me to heed their words, for I had surrounded myself with people who constantly told me that I'd soon be a star—that I had one of the best voices they had ever heard. To all who told me to return to the feet of Jesus, I simply replied, "If God wants me to return, He Himself will have to ask me to do so."

This went on for over three years, and after traveling back and forth between the Dominican Republic and the United States, I found myself in the city of Lawrence, Massachusetts, singing alongside artists Luis Vargas and Luis Segura. The concert was a great success, performed to a full house. I remember singing and dancing my heart out, giving my fans a performance well worth their money. Then, a week after the concert, as I lay in my bed, I had a revelation that would change my life.

I dreamed that I was at the same concert hall and on the same stage where I had just performed my latest concert. I began to sing and dance, and all the people were having a great time singing the lyrics along with me. As I kept singing, the entire crowd suddenly disappeared, and in their place was a very bright-white snow. I was astonished when I saw this, and I stopped singing and walked to the edge of the scene to get a closer look at what had just taken place.

As I reached the edge of the snow, it disappeared suddenly, and in its place once more appeared a multitude of people, dressed in robes as white and bright as the snow I had previously seen. All the people were walking forward in a straight line, heading west. I jumped off the stage and began to walk, with the multitude on my right side, in the same direction they were heading. After walking for a few hours, I finally reached the front of the line, where thousands upon ten thousands of people were standing in anticipation of something and someone.

I stood a few meters away from the throng, as I was interested in knowing what these people were doing there—and who or what they were waiting for. As I watched them, I saw a man walking in my direction. As I looked at him, I could not speak or even open my mouth. I recognized him immediately. It was Jesus! I knew Him to be Jesus!

When He reached me, He looked at me intently. It was then that I noticed that, unlike everyone else, I had no white robes on. With a voice of commanding authority, Jesus asked me, "What are you doing here?" I answered, "Lord, I am singing." Tenderly, Jesus replied, "Cease what you are doing and come; be a light for my people."

Then Jesus began to sing a song that I had written a long time ago, one that a friend who was a Christian singer had recorded. The Lord sang the following words: "Come; join God's people. Be the light in the darkness. Come; serve Christ the Savior, and He shall grant you heavenly treasures. Come; waste not your time! Come; many are the souls that perish that know not God's great love. Come, my friend. Come and serve the Lord."

After that, I left the music and entertainment industry, never to return. Looking back at my experience and my behavior, I can see that God has a wonderful sense of humor. All my brethren who had asked me to return to Christ—and to whom I had replied, "If God wants me to return, He Himself will have to ask me to do so"—now marvel at how Christ appeared to me in a vision. He Himself called me back to His way, His truth, and His kingdom.

We all go ways that are separate from God at times in our lives. In many cases, such as mine, God Himself brings us back to His feet. The Lord is always at His work, calling us and offering us His love and protection. It is very important that we listen to His voice. God can call us, but in the end, He cannot respond for us.

"'Even now,' declares the LORD, 'return to me with all your heart, with fasting and weeping and mourning'" (Joel 2:12 NIV).

Make No False Promises

"When you vow a vow to God, do not delay paying it, for he has no pleasure in fools. Pay what you vow. It is better that you should not vow than that you should vow and not pay. Let not your mouth lead you into sin, and do not say before the messenger that it was a mistake. Why should God be angry at your voice and destroy the work of your hands?" (Ecclesiastes 5:4–6 ESV).

In 1999 while attending college, I prayed to God and promised Him that if He blessed me with a car, I would more readily seek Him and attend church. At the time, my mother and siblings were members of the Seventh Day Adventist church. In April of that same year, by the grace of God, I was able to acquire my first car for a very cheap price: a 1984 Honda Accord. Most times, I had to pray before trying to start the car, hoping that it would turn on, but it was all I could afford then. Naturally, I took my car out as often as I could, and I totally forgot—or, more accurately, I disregarded—my end of the bargain.

My own mother reminded me of my promise on many occasions, stating that since God had been faithful to me, I should be faithful to Him in kind. But I simply complied with her requests in word only, and then I went about doing my own thing.

Four months after acquiring the car, on a Saturday morning in August, I was headed to work in the town of Nyack when I had a car accident. Only by God's grace was I okay, though I could not say the same for the state of my car. Roughly an hour after the incident, my mother called me, and I heard the concern in her voice. "Are you all right? she asked. "How bad was the accident?"

I was awestruck, as I had not called or told anyone about the incident. "What?" I asked. "How did you know about my accident?"

She answered, "An hour ago, as I was praying, the Lord revealed to me that you had been in an accident, and He sends you a message." She then quoted from Ecclesiastes 5: "It is better not to make a vow than to make one and not fulfill it. Do not let your mouth lead you into sin. And do not protest to the temple messenger, 'My vow was a mistake.' Why should God be angry at what you say and destroy the work of your hands?"

After hearing such a message, I understood this to be a calling and a serious warning from God. He is a faithful God, and in the same manner, He calls us to be faithful also, especially to what we promise Him. It is better not to promise than to promise and not fulfill our word, says the Lord. From that day on, I began to seek the Lord, asking Him for understanding of His Word.

Just like me, there are many others who have made a promise to the Lord but who have forgotten about it because of life's many problems. It is my prayer that we will remember our pacts with the Lord, since He expects us to do what we promise. Even if it is an old promise or something that happened decades ago, God still expects us to be faithful, especially with our time and money—but more importantly, with our hearts.

"'For I know the plans I have for you,' declares the LORD, 'plans to prosper you and not to harm you, plans to give you hope and a future'" (Jeremiah 29:11 NIV).

An Open Door

"I know all the things you do, and I have opened a door for you that no one can close. You have little strength, yet you obeyed my word and did not deny me" (Revelation 3:8 NLT).

Not too long ago, I met an Adventist canvasser who was selling a series of videos called *Ancient Secrets of the Bible*, which I was interested in acquiring. We agreed on a two-payment plan of $125 each for the set, where I would give him the first payment when he delivered the videos, and I would make the second payment a month after the first installment.

Shortly after I had received the videos and had paid the first installment, I became extremely busy at work. Two months passed, and I had yet to make my second payment to the canvasser as we had agreed, though I was constantly mindful of making that payment. Four months after I had acquired the video series, I was heading to work on a Tuesday morning. I looked at the clock, and it said 7:20 a.m., so I thought I would go to visit the canvasser and bring him the remaining money I owed.

The canvasser lived in an area of New York City where parking is nearly impossible to come by, especially at such early hours of the morning. On top of that, his building does not have an intercom system to ring the apartment bell, meaning that the only way to get in is to have the key that opens the front entrance—unless, by some miracle, someone is walking out while you are waiting to get in. When I made the decision to go and make my final payment, I began to pray. I asked God, first, to find or reserve me a parking spot, and second, to send someone down to the entrance so I could get into the building, make my payment, and get to work on time.

When I arrived at the block where the building was located, I noticed that there were no parking spaces available, so I closed my eyes and prayed again, asking for God's mercy. When I opened my eyes, I saw a car moving out three street blocks ahead, so I quickly made my way over and parked my car.

After parking the car, I prayed again to thank God for His provision, and then I asked for a way to enter the building as quickly as possible. When I exited the car, I noticed in the middle of the road a key-holder with three keys on it. At first I thought nothing of it, but I felt compelled to pick them up.

When I arrived at the building, I waited outside for three minutes, hoping that someone would exit or enter so I could get in. Suddenly I heard the voice of God say, "What are you waiting for? I gave you the keys. Go in!"

Scared, with trembling hands, I quickly took the keys out and put one in the door. I was speechless to discover that those keys were for that door. When I went up to the canvasser's apartment, I told him what God had just done for me, how He had acted in a supernatural manner. We both prayed and gave glory to God, for He is good, and His mercy and grace endure for generations.

As we often pray for God to grant us a request or help us solve difficulties, let us remember that God is working in our favor. Many times, He may not answer in the way we are hoping or in the time we are expecting. Nevertheless, we need to trust that His timing is perfect and that He knows the end from the beginning. Therefore, let us trust His judgments and pray that His will be done in our lives.

I'd Rather Have Jesus

"So you must live as God's obedient children. Don't slip back into your old ways of living to satisfy your own desires. You didn't know any better then" (1 Peter 1:14 NLT).

Some time ago, I was talking with an old friend, who asked me for advice concerning some Latin bachata songs. This friend—we'll call him Raff—asked me the procedure for submitting his songs to a famous singer who had asked to hear his compositions. After we discussed the steps he needed to take, he was enthusiastic, for this was a great opportunity for him.

My wife and mother-in-law were present while my friend and I were talking, and they encouraged me to submit some of my songs to be considered also. They were looking at the financial benefits that producing top-of-the-charts songs could bring. Early in the conversation, I told them no, but immediately beautiful words began flowing through my head—words that I could use to write some very good lyrics. I was tempted to get a pen and paper to write down my emotions and thoughts for that purpose. Minutes later, I fell asleep on the couch, and the following scene was before me:

I was taken up on a hill, where a group of people was waiting for me, and they greeted me happily. Upon arriving, they passed me a microphone and said, "Preach!" When I looked before me, I saw below the hill a crowd of thousands upon thousands, all waiting to hear what message I had. As soon as I began to speak, I saw a group of one hundred people give their lives to Christ. As I kept speaking, I saw that the entire throng present gave their lives to the service of Christ. All were praising God for the words I had taken to them and for the salvation they had received through Jesus Christ.

When I stopped talking, God once more confirmed my purpose and calling. He reminded me of the reason He had previously called me to leave the world behind and follow Christ: to be a light for His people. I do not claim to be the light, but the Word of God, which I carry, *is* the light, and if I live what I preach from the Word of God, then all will see the light in me. It is written in Psalm 119:105 (NLT): "Your word is a light to my feet, and a light to my path."

I am sure that there are many nonbelievers and skeptics, who, upon reading these words, might find excuses for my stories, or simply chalk them up to pure coincidence.

Nevertheless, when I read the Word of God, when I see that Word in action, how can I not believe?

When I have been in dire need and have come before my heavenly Father to ask for an answer, and I get an immediate response, how can that be just a coincidence? I watch a sunset and feel a sense of my own utter insignificance, and I realize that this world is but a tiny grain in the sandy shores of the universe. When I feel this wonder, I want to praise something that must be much higher than me. How is it possible that these feelings of wonder are ingrained in my soul?

I have spoken honest words about my personal experiences. In the end, however, the choice is ours as to whether we will believe or not believe. I have made my choice based on what I have lived, and they are but a few of the reasons why I believe!

3

Keeping Your Peace

My Deliverer

"So he said to me, 'This is the word of the Lord to Zerubbabel: "Not by might nor by power, but by my Spirit," says the Lord Almighty'" (Zechariah 4:6 NIV).

Like most Christians, one of my greatest weaknesses is my lack of faith. Though Christ once said that if our faith were as small as a mustard seed, we would command the mountains to move from one place to another, and they would move, we often tend to focus more on the severity of the problem at hand than on the greatness of God. Slowly I have come to learn that, instead of telling God how great my problems are, I should tell my problems how great my God is!

On one occasion, as I drove home with my wife and two children, a driver behind me began to honk his car horn as though enraged with me. The road we drove along had only one lane going in each direction, with a fire lane between them. I drove five miles over the allotted speed limit, but I guess the driver was in a tremendous hurry to get to his destination. Pulling his car next to mine—in the fire lane, mind you—he hurled insults at me.

I won't lie. I wanted to respond in kind, but given that my wife and children were spectating, anticipating my reaction, I instead took a deep breath and said, "Lord, you know I've not done anything against this individual to cause him to hurl insults at me. Your Word says that vengeance belongs to the Lord, so I leave this in your hands." Not even ten seconds after my prayer, the driver collided with a wall.

My wife and I were in shocked by what had happened, and we looked to see if we could help this man in any way. We did not want to be happy at his misfortune, but at the same time, we understood that God guards those He loves, as stated in Psalm 17:8 (KJV): "Keep me as the apple of the eye, hide me under the shadow of thy wings."

God will always fight our battles when we rely on Him to do so. His mighty Spirit is ready and willing to defend us in our times of trouble. Let us bring our problems to His feet, and God will wipe away all tears from our eyes.

"The angel of the LORD encamps around those who fear him, and he delivers them" (Psalm 34:7 NIV).

4

Angels among Us

You Might Be an Angel

"Be not forgetful to entertain strangers: for thereby some have entertained angels unawares" (Hebrews 13:2 KJV).

An angel is a messenger of or for God, a being of light that is at the Almighty's disposal and service. When we think of angels, we usually imagine them as beings surrounded by God's glory and radiance, dressed in fine, white linen, having wings on their backs. However, the Bible teaches us that many times the angels dispose of their heavenly majesty and take up human form so that they may deliver a message that would otherwise be undeliverable in their glorious state.

In the book of Joshua, we can see a very good example of an angel appearing as a man. "Now when Joshua was near Jericho, he looked up and saw a man standing in front of him with a drawn sword in his hand. Joshua went up to him and asked, 'Are you for us or for our enemies?'" (Joshua 5:13 NIV).

In Hebrews 13:2, the Word of God tells us, "Do not neglect to show hospitality to strangers, for by this some have entertained angels without knowing it."

It is important to note that humans on earth are not actual angels, but we are sometimes chosen by God to do the work of angels or to be His messengers.

For example, John the Baptist was not the personification of Elijah, but in Matthew 17:10–13, Jesus referred to John the Baptist as Elijah, meaning that he was *like* Elijah, bringing a message of warning and repentance.

In January of 2014, the year started with a snowstorm. Though my wife and I lived in Connecticut, we still worked in New York City. It was a Thursday, and the forecast warned of snow later on in the day. Angie was done working by 3:00 p.m., so she went to pick up the kids from the parochial school they attended. After she got the kids, she waited around for me to be done at 5:00 p.m. so that we could embark homeward.

At 5:30, seeing that I was taking so long to arrive, Angie grew weary of waiting. She decided to leave so that the storm would not catch her on the drive back home. Around 6:00 p.m., I called her cell, and she told me she had left. I will not lie: I was rather angry at that moment, because she had left me behind. I asked her to turn back, as she's not used to driving in the snow, and I waited until 6:30 p.m. for her return. When I realized that she was not returning, I called her again to make sure that she and the kids were fine. She was already over thirty minutes into her journey home.

In fear for their safety, I prayed and then decided to head home myself. The entire drive home was a battle between man and Mother Nature, as my car was nearly as unfit for snow as my wife's car. I was constantly asking God for travel mercies and for His protection.

At 7:15 p.m., I called Angie's cell again. My eldest son, Juan Marcos, answered and told me that they had arrived in the town where we lived. I was still worried for their safety, as we lived atop a hill, which I knew my wife's car was incapable of climbing in this extreme weather. I kept praying and driving cautiously, because the amount of snow on the road would not allow for speedy travel.

Upon arriving in our town, I realized that it would be nearly impossible for my car to make it up the hill. It took me twelve minutes to get past a spot that would've taken only four to five seconds on a regular snowless day, for my car slipped as though it was on an ice rink.

I kept driving up the hill, little by little, and when I was halfway up, I saw a woman outside her car, signaling for help. When I stopped, I realized that it was Angie. She was very surprised to see me, since she was unaware that I had also driven home rather than staying at my mother's house in the Bronx. Upon seeing me, she could not stop crying. She said, "I've been trying for more than twenty minutes to get the car up over the hill, but I haven't been able to. The car kept slipping, and I almost had an accident, and the kids are crying scared."

She continued, "You will never believe what I have to tell you. You are the last person I expected to see at this moment. Just a few seconds ago, I was crying and filled with regret for not listening to you when you suggested we stay in the Bronx for the night, and so I prayed. I said, 'Lord, please have compassion on me and my children. I beg you to send forth an angel to help us. I am desperate, and my children are scared. Send me an angel, Lord.' After praying, I got out of the car and immediately saw a car coming. And now I can't believe that it's you whom God sent."

After she told me her story, all of my anger dissipated at once. I knew then that God had a purpose for her leaving ahead of me so abruptly, and that purpose was to show me that we are all capable of doing the work of an angel. We can all be touched by the Spirit of God that we might do whatever He calls us to do, but in the end, we hold the choice as to whether or not we will answer the call. You can be an angel too!

Giving Is a Blessing

"Heal the sick, raise the dead, cleanse the lepers and cast out demons. Freely you have received, freely give" (Matthew 10:8 NKJV).

I've always known giving to be an utmost privilege, and I've seen this privilege enacted many times before my own eyes in my own life. God's promises are clear and very effective regarding a heart that gives happily and freely. We often think of giving as offering material things. However, a simple smile can make a change in someone's life.

Throughout God's Word, we often see Him demanding that His people help their fellow man, and His command is much more than just a simple request or suggestion. Mark 10:21 (NIV) says, "Jesus looked at him and loved him. 'One thing you lack,' he said. 'Go, sell everything you have and give to the poor, and you will have treasure in heaven. Then come, follow me.'"

God's people need to better understand the blessing involved in the concept of giving, for when that day comes when God Himself is manifested to us, we shall receive blessing upon blessing and abundant grace.

In Malachi 3:10 (NIV), we find the following promise: "'Bring the whole tithe into the storehouse, so that there may be food in My house, and test Me now in this,' says the Lord of hosts, 'if I will not open for you the windows of heaven, and pour out for you blessing until it overflows.'" It is rather evident that giving is a blessing indeed!

A few months ago, I felt the need in my heart to help some friends who were visiting the United States and were going through a very tough time. I am not a person who possesses many resources, but I have counted on God's plentiful provision to provide for my every need. Looking at the amount of money that I had in hand, I decided to give them all that I had at that moment, which was a hundred dollars. After giving the money away, I realized that I had forgotten to put gas in my car to make it back home. Upon remembering this, I prayed to God to supply my present need according to His riches in glory. Rather than worrying about the situation, I decided to trust in Him, knowing that He can do all things.

Roughly four hours later, I met up with a friend whom I had not seen in ages. We were happy to see each other after such a long time. When the time came to go our separate ways, she gave me her hand and said, "Merry Christmas." When she took her hand away, I noticed that she had left me a folded envelope, which I thought might be a Christmas card. I waited for her to leave before I opened it, but when I did, I found $300 inside.

I could not believe my eyes. I had just received much more than I had given, far more than I needed to fill my gas tank. God's goodness and grace are undeserved and amazing. It reminds me of the verse found in Matthew 6:25 (NIV): "For this reason I say unto you, do not be worried about your life as to what you will eat or what you will drink; nor for your body, as to what you will put on. Is not life more than food and the body more than clothing?"

Our heavenly Father is an amazing provider. I pray every day that He will create in me the desire to give, since giving is an amazing privilege. For those who profess to love Christ, giving should come naturally, with the sole purpose of doing what the Lord would do if He was in that same situation. It is even more important that we always give with a pure heart, not expecting anything in return. Even so, I compare giving with making a deposit in my heavenly bank account.

Send Me, O Lord

"For he will command his angels concerning you to guard you in all your ways; they will lift you up in their hands" (Psalm 91:11–12 NIV).

It saddens my heart to see both old and young suffer from sickness and pain. Our hospitals are full of men, women, and children who desperately cry in anguish because of their conditions. Today, I want you to remember that we are not alone and that God is watching over you.

My childhood was a very difficult one. I had a condition known as thrombocytopenia. This is caused when the blood does not have enough platelets to clump together and plug holes in open blood vessels to stop bleeding. I used to bleed huge amounts of blood through my mouth and nose on a daily basis. There was so much bleeding that, by the time I was four years old, dark spots covered my whole body. To make matters worse, I was admitted to the hospital with severe pulmonary problems after getting pneumonia. Days later, I was also diagnosed with measles.

Being very poor, my parents were extremely sad, not knowing where they would get the money to pay for my treatment. Back in the Dominican Republic, if you did not have the money to pay the hospital, they would let you die without even seeing you.

When the doctor informed my father of my condition and what the cost would be, my father's mind was lost in deep thought. The hospital cost would exceed thirty Dominican pesos, which was more money than he had seen at any one time in his life. Back in the early 1980s, the Dominican peso was a very strong currency, and a day's wage was between one and two pesos.

After delivering the news, the doctor walked away, leaving my father wondering what he could do or where he could get the money necessary to cover the expenses. As he stared at a green mountain from the hospital's balcony, a man put his hand on my father's shoulder and asked him, "How are you today?"

"Fine," my father replied.

"Is everything all right?" the man asked.

"Yes, it is all fine," my father said. "I'm just here praying and looking at the mountain."

"Don't think too hard," the man told him. Then he pulled his wallet out of his jacket and handed a fifty-peso bill to my father. "Do what you need to do," he told him.

My father did not know what to do or what to say, and he started to cry. The man walked away, saying that everything would be fine.

I have seen the hand of God in my life since my early childhood. I know that God has been there for me every step of the way. How can I not do His will?

I know that there are angels among us who do God's will and go where God sends them. When my father told me this story, I broke down in tears. Not only did God answer his prayer while he was still observing the mountain, but He also completely healed me from my sickness. I don't want to focus too much on the sickness or the fact that I was healed, for it is my quest to convince people that we must listen to God's voice when He speaks. Then we must do His will, wherever He might send us.

Let us be a blessing to others—just as this stranger was to my father—since God commands us to give as freely as we have received. We can all do the work of an angel!

5

God Always Works for the Good

The Lord Knows Why

"Trust in the LORD with all your heart and lean not on your own understanding; in all your ways submit to him, and he will make your paths straight" (Proverbs 3:5–6 NIV).

Throughout the years, I have noticed that God indeed knows best, and only He is capable of looking into the future. On various occasions when I decided to drive out to work, something happened at home that impeded my timely departure so I couldn't leave when I intended to. On many of those occasions, I tended to become angry with my wife, Angie, as I do not like to arrive anywhere late. I think punctuality is an obsession of mine. I have discovered, however, that there is a reason and purpose for everything that occurs in my life. God allows certain situations that may discomfort me, but in the end, the discomfort I endure is for my greater good.

On many of my drives to work, I have witnessed a great number of accidents that occurred mere minutes before I drove by that specific place. If I had left my house when I'd intended to do so, I probably would have been another statistic instead of a witness.

As we face obstacles in life—and even when we face problems that are supposed to be small but somehow escalate and become serious issues—let us remember that God is in charge. When our kids take five extra minutes preparing for church, when our wives put on too much makeup and have to spend time doing it over, or when we simply spill juice or coffee on our shirts, this is God somehow holding us back to protect us from trouble.

"We have nothing to fear for the future, except as we shall forget the way the Lord has led us and His teaching in our past history" (Ellen Gould Harmon White, *Life Sketches of Ellen G. White* [Pacific Press Publishing Association, 1902], 196).

God Heals and Saves

"He himself bore our sins in his body on the tree, that we might die to sin and live to righteousness. By his wounds you have been healed" (1 Peter 2:24 ESV).

My heart lives in constant joy, because I know that my God listens and answers all our prayers if we ask in faith. There is nothing He will not do for those who love Him and serve Him with all their hearts.

In 2007 my grandfather on my mother's side was in a delicate state of health. At eighty-nine years of age, his body was quite fragile, and his heart and lung problems had him at the final phase of his life. By July his health took an extreme turn for the worse, to the point that the doctors decided to send him home that he might spend his last days with his family and loved ones. Upon receiving this news, I was greatly distressed and saddened, and in my anguish, I asked the Lord to allow me to see him and to preserve his life until I could go to him in the Dominican Republic.

That same day, I received news that my grandfather had finally been able to eat something. Slowly, his health began to improve, and finally, in the summer of the following year, God granted me the opportunity to travel to the Dominican Republic and see him. I do not want to spend too much time telling you about this story, because many stories of this nature are merely natural coincidences. I, on the other hand, am fully convinced that this was God's providence. After my visit, my grandfather lived another four years before God brought him to rest until His second coming.

This story may be similar to that of many men and women who are pleading in anguish over their own health problems or those of a loved one. God listens to our prayers when we ask with the assurance that He will act in our favor. It is also very important to mention that many times God answers a prayer in a way different from the way we are expecting. This means that sometimes He may answer by immediately granting our petition, or He may ask us to wait. Either way, we must trust that, in the end, He is doing what is in our best interest.

I was very humbled that God answered my prayer because of His grace and mercy. Let our lives be filled with prayers and songs to glorify God's name. The Lord is our healer and the one who can cure the body and the soul. There is nothing he will not do for us, if we ask in faith in the perfect name of Jesus, our Lord and Savior.

Look at this beautiful quote from Ellen G. White: "No man is safe for a day or an hour without prayer" (Ellen Gould Harmon White, *The Great Controversy,* [Pacific Press Publishing Association, 1870]).

6

God Heals

The Prayer of the Just

"Is anyone among you sick? Then he must call for the elders of the church and they are to pray over him, anointing him with oil in the name of the Lord; and the prayer offered in faith will restore the one who is sick, and the Lord will raise him up, and if he has committed sins, they will be forgiven him" (James 5:14–15 NASB).

For most of my life, I have been in very good health. I have only been hospitalized once before, when I still was a baby. However, things can change quickly. In the blink of an eye, we can find ourselves in very unexpected situations. Whatever the case may be, I know that I can always come to Jesus.

One September night, after eating dinner with my family, I went to bed around 10:30 p.m. or so. Around 2:00 a.m., I woke up from pain in my back and abdomen, which I had not experienced prior to that moment. Angie woke up after hearing my laments of discomfort, and she drove me to the nearest emergency room. Upon arriving at St. Mary's Hospital, I was admitted immediately.

I had kidney stones—a lot of kidney stones, apparently, as I was hospitalized for three days and needed surgery to extract a stone that had fallen into my urinary tract and was too big to pass. Little by little, I began to get better, and thankfully, I started to *feel* better as well. Two months later, I had a similar episode, and once again, I found myself back in the emergency room. This time I was in and out of the hospital for quite a while.

In January of the following year, my urologist decided to perform laser surgery to break up two of the nine stones that were left in both of my kidneys. The stones were too large when passing, so you can imagine my pain. A few days after said surgery, and after many visits to the emergency room, a pastor friend of mine called to pray with and for me. He spoke a powerful prayer, entrusting me to the hands of Jesus that He might grant me healing. We proclaimed that the stones would all pass through, and that my pain would cease.

Two hours after the prayer, I felt the need to urinate. Immediately, to my great surprise, large stones passed through with the urine, and they continued to do so for the next two days, after which my pain ceased all at once.

I am convinced that God is faithful to His promises. In His Word, He declares that He will listen to our prayers and heal our bodies. Jesus suffered our sickness so that through Him we could all be healed. Isn't that an amazing promise?

Of course, if anyone falls sick, he ought to seek medical attention. But we must never forget that the most important thing we should do is to seek, through prayer and supplication, the face of the one who can do all things, who can heal the body and the soul. God knows our weaknesses, as He is our creator. He is the God who heals and saves, and He is coming for us soon. He has healed me and saved me, and can do the same for all of us, if we ask in prayer.

If we or our family members are sick, we should repeat these words, and we will see God's power at work:

Heavenly Father, thank you that you are my Creator, my refuge, and my fortress. I believe in You, and I believe that You have the power to heal. Please, O Lord, heal my body and my soul, and please remember me when You come in glory with Your holy angels. I make this prayer, not because I am worthy, but because of the precious blood of Jesus, who is our Lord and Savior. In His name I pray, amen.

7

The Favor of God

Miracle at Birth

"Before I formed you in the womb I knew you, and before you were born I consecrated you; I appointed you a prophet to the nations" (Jeremiah 1:5 ESV).

In April of 2002, a mere few months after my wife and I had gotten married, we had the wonderful surprise of learning that we would be having our first child. We both were ecstatic about this news, though I will confess that, being only twenty-two years old, I was scared out of my mind at the same time. As the months flew by, we prepared for the baby's arrival, anticipating that the birth of this child would bring Angie and me closer to each other and would give us immeasurable happiness. He was to be born at the end of December.

In mid-October, Angie began to experience some pain and contractions, which were normal at this time in her pregnancy. However, these labor pains got worse and worse as the days carried on. On the October 30, Angie's contractions were insufferable, so we decided to go to the hospital. When we arrived at the ER, a nurse quickly intervened and took Angie to the delivery room.

Nerves and worry overwhelmed me and took me hostage at that moment, and my thoughts were on the fact that my son would be born prematurely at seven months. I pleaded my case before God, begging the Lord of Hosts for mercy on behalf of my child. I knew that children born prematurely had plenty of complications, and a great majority of them lost the battle.

In the early hours of October 31, our son was born. We named Juan Marcos, after the author of the gospel of Mark in the Bible. He was born at four pounds, and being premature, he was to remain in the hospital a few days for observation. When we questioned the doctor about our son's premature birth, he readily answered us. "The child is alive through a miracle of nature," he said. "His umbilical chord was wrapped around his neck. Had he remained in the womb more than another week, he would have died, asphyxiated."

I learned that we must understand that God's plan is always in our favor. Even when our surroundings grow dark, and things do not seem to go our way, we must take it on faith and trust that God is choosing the outcome that is best for us.

Today, as I see how Juan Marcos has grown both physically and emotionally, I marvel at God's mercy and love. Every time I receive a letter from the honor roll society at his school, and every time he earns an award for working hard, I praise God for the miracle that He performed a little over ten years ago. "For the LORD is good and his love endures forever; his faithfulness continues through all generations" (Psalm 100:5 NIV).

Blessings in the Trials

"Now an angel of the Lord said to Philip, 'Go south to the road—the desert road—that goes down from Jerusalem to Gaza.' So he started out, and on his way he met an Ethiopian eunuch, an important official in charge of all the treasury of the Kandake [which means "queen of the Ethiopians"]. This man had gone to Jerusalem to worship and on his way home was sitting in his chariot reading the Book of Isaiah the prophet. The Spirit told Philip, 'Go to that chariot and stay near it'" (Acts 8:26–29 NIV).

Recently, I was invited to the state of Georgia to give a conference to young adults regarding the importance of being like Jesus in today's society. Right from the initial planning, the Devil tried, in many different ways, to persuade me not to go. I kept my mind in constant prayer for God's will to be done and for His name to be glorified during my stay in Atlanta.

The conference was to start on a Friday night, so I decided to fly there from New York on the morning of that same Friday. My flight was delayed by two hours due to inclement weather. As I sat in the waiting area, I saw a young woman who looked very worried and distressed. In my spirit, I prayed for her and asked the good Lord to meet whatever need she might have, be it financial, emotional, or spiritual.

Sometime later, we boarded the plane, and I discovered that the young woman's seat was right next to mine. As I always do, I introduced myself as a Christian minister, not only to help me be on my best behavior at all times, since I must represent Christ before others, but because it will also shape others' behavior around me. As she started talking, she asked me why I believed in God and what the difference was between Christianity and other religions.

I explained to her that Christianity was not simply a religion but rather a lifestyle. I said that it was a life full of joy—unlike the joy expressed by the world—and that Christian joy came from knowing Jesus and what He had done and was still doing for me. I also explained to her that as a believer I held the hope that one day soon, Jesus, who had been crucified and had risen again, was coming back from His heavenly dwelling to take us home with Him. We spoke for the duration of the flight, until we arrived at Charlotte, North Carolina. As we said goodbye, she told me that she had not been to a church in several years, but starting that same weekend, she would attend church and ask about Bible studies.

After twenty minutes in North Carolina, my next flight, which would take me to Atlanta, began to board. When we arrived in Atlanta, I was surprised to learn that my suitcase had not made it onto my flight. Many other passengers were annoyed and started to argue and complain to the airline attendant. One by one, we all made our way to a small office to report that our bags had not arrived with our flight. I had nothing else with me except my Bible, which I had decided to take out of my suitcase before boarding the flight in Newark.

When I walked into the small office, the airport attendant asked me, "Are you going to scream at me also?"

"Why?" I replied. "I understand that God allows things for a reason, and I believe I know why this happened."

"Why?" she asked.

"I believe that I am here so you can be saved."

We spoke for almost an hour. I told her that I had come to Georgia to preach the Word of God to young people like her and to help them be more like Jesus. She was very interested. A little less than forty minutes later, this young woman was accepting Jesus as her personal Savior.

I did not get my suitcase until the evening of the next day, but God's purpose was fulfilled, and those who were destined to be saved came to His feet in repentance. Despite all these "inconveniences" that seemed to deter me from getting to the place where I was to share God's Word, God showed me that His timing, not mine, is best. These obstacles were not an impedance to my arrival, but rather they were mere pauses that God allowed so that I might share His salvation with others.

It is my hope that we can all let go of our frustrations when things do not seem to go our way, that instead we will stop and think, "How can I do God's work while I wait on my own plans?"

8

Marriage

Unequally Yoked

"That is why a man leaves his father and mother and is united to his wife, and they become one flesh" (Genesis 2:24 NIV).

Throughout the Old and New Testaments, we see that God is jealous for His people. On many occasions, God warned them not to marry people who did not share the same faith as theirs. One of the many reasons why the Lord opposed such unions was the fact that many people abandoned their faith after marrying a nonbeliever.

This was the case of King Ahab, who married Jezebel, a foreign woman, and later introduced the land of Israel to the worship of Baal, a foreign god who had no eyes to see or mouth to speak.

In 1 Kings 16:31 (GWT), we read: "It wasn't enough that he committed the same sins as Jeroboam (Nebat's son).

He also married Jezebel, daughter of King Ethbaal of Sidon. Ahab then served and worshiped Baal."

Today, according to the American Psychological Association's website (www.apa.org), between 40 and 50 percent of marriages in the United States end in divorce, which, of course, is a rather alarming statistic, as it shows the decline in social, political, and religious morals in the United States.

Let me be clear about something. I am a law-abiding American citizen in good standing, and I have grown to love this country as much as my native Dominican Republic. Nevertheless, it saddens me to see so many homes and children affected by such a high divorce rate.

It is impossible to study the concept of being unequally yoked without first reading God's admonishments given throughout history. To many people, being unequally yoked means being married to someone from a different race or financial status. However, the truth is that being unequally yoked, according to the Word of God, is the union of a Jehovah-worshipper with someone who worships a different god or gods.

This is what God commanded the Israelites as He delivered them out of Egypt: "Furthermore, you shall not intermarry with them; you shall not give your daughters to their sons, nor shall you take their daughters for your sons. For they will turn your sons away from following Me to serve other gods; then the anger of the Lord will be kindled against you and He will quickly destroy you" (Deuteronomy 7:3–4 NASB).

Of course, God was speaking to the sons of Jacob, instructing them on how they ought to live in the new land that He had given them. Marrying or having a relationship with someone of a different faith is nothing more than an obstruction to our serving and obeying God as He has required us to do. God's children must trust Him as their sovereign Lord, knowing that they can trust Him to help them make the correct choices when making their own decisions.

God says, "Before I formed you in the womb I knew you, and before you were born, I consecrated you; I appointed you a prophet to the nations" (Jeremiah 1:5). God assures us that He knew us even before He formed us in our mother's womb. How, then, can we not trust that He knows what is best for us?

When Angie was fourteen years old, it was normal for children to begin being attracted to the opposite sex. Her peers constantly made fun of her for not having a "little boyfriend" or someone who was interested in her. One day while she was being mocked at school, Angie told the other kids that she did have a boyfriend. The other kids were surprised when they heard this, and they readily demanded the name of this mysterious person. Angie was nervous and did not know what to say, for she was making the whole thing up to avoid the mockery and teasing. "Juan Bautista," she answered without thinking.

Although not all the other students believed her, it did dissipate the mocking and teasing for some time.

When Angie told me about the kids teasing her about a boyfriend, I laughed a little. I know how cruel children can be to each other. But when Angie told me the name of her "imaginary boyfriend," my laughter turned to shock. Of course, she told me this story two years into our marriage, and even so, the story surprised me.

The name given to me when I was born was Juan de Dios Nunez Bautista. Nuñez is my father's last name, and Bautista is my mother's maiden name, but as I was growing up, my friends jokingly called me Juan Bautista, or "John the Baptist."

Many people might see this story as a mere coincidence, but it is impossible for me not to feel wonder and surprise about the way God acts in my life. Knowing that God chose me for my wife, and that He chose Angie for me, fills me with such joy, even to this day!

Every day, I live in the fear of the Lord so that I can make Angie happy, as this is what I know to be God's will for me. I am certain that God wants to help us all choose whom we will marry—just as He did for me. Can you imagine what it would do for the divorce rate around the world if we chose to listen to God's voice and guidance?

Now, I encourage those who are already married—especially to someone who does not share your faith—to continue to pray that your partner will accept God's call for his or her salvation. I have seen many people's prayers answered, with their partners and children coming to the feet of Christ.

There is a beautiful hymn—one of my favorites, actually—that has helped me in my daily life. The words go like this: "I want what it is that you want for me, whatever you ask me to do. For I know you know what is best. I want what you would want."

This should be our song, day by day. We should be asking God for His will to be done in our lives—not just in choosing the person we will marry but in every important decision we make.

9

Reasons for Everything

Salvation in Jail

"Also I heard the voice of the Lord, saying, 'Whom shall I send, and who will go for us?' Then said I, 'Here am I; send me'" (Isaiah 6:8 Wycliffe).

Some years ago, while I was driving in the city of New York, I was stopped by a police officer because one of my taillights was out. As the officer approached my car, he asked, "Do you know why I stopped you?"

"No, officer," I replied.

"Your left taillight is broken," he said. He immediately asked for my driver's license and my registration, which I readily made available to him. As he returned to his vehicle, he asked me to step out of my car. I could not understand what was happening. He told me, "Mr. Bautista, you are being arrested because your driver's license has been expired for over a month, and it is illegal to drive with an expired license."

At that moment, my whole world came crumbling down. Prior to that incident, I'd never had any problems with the law. This would be a devastating blow for me and my family, I thought.

When I was taken to one of the jail cells, I simply went and sat in a corner. All I could do at that moment was pray to God. Disgraced and full of shame, I couldn't believe that I hadn't noticed that my license had expired. I asked God to show me any lesson I was to learn from all this, and I asked Him to guide me through the ordeal. Since the arrest took place on a Friday night, this meant that I would have to wait until Monday to see a judge. Unfortunately, it also meant three shameful days in jail under terrible conditions.

When day two came around, I was greatly surprised to see one of my former students being escorted to the same jail cell that I was in. As soon as he saw me, he started to cry. "Why are you here?" I asked.

With his eyes full of tears, he responded, saying, "I was caught in an armed robbery." At that moment, I cried with him, for I had known him since he was in the fourth grade. It hurt me to see him now, struggling through life as an adult.

Immediately I understood that something good would come out of my negligence. I understood God's plan for me in being there. God had used my neglect to send me to bring salvation to this young man by preaching the name of Jesus to him.

As I explained Scripture to him, he asked several questions regarding pain and suffering, which I clarified for him. By the end of that day, this young man had accepted Jesus as his personal Savior and was willing to walk God's way. Early on Monday morning, only hours after he had received Jesus, I was taken to see a judge, who released me without filing any charges.

Many times we pray, just as the prophet Isaiah did, and ask God to send us and to use us for His glory. The question is, are we sure that we are willing to go through pain and suffering, to endure hunger and thirst, in order to do God's work?

Now that you have read this story, it is my prayer that you will be even more motivated to trust God's plan for you, remembering that all things work out for the best interest of all God's children. God may send us to places where we do not want to go, to do things that we do not want to do. But we must take it on faith that the task He entrusts to us is for our benefit.

Put yourself in His hands, and let Him use you in any way He desires, because He knows your true potential for His glory and honor.

10

Do Unto Others

Do Unto Others

"So whatever you wish that others would do to you, do also to them, for this is the Law and the Prophets" (Matthew 7:12 ESV).

What a privilege it is to serve and to work on behalf of others, and what an amazing feeling it is to be treated with love and respect by our colleagues and friends. Loving one another is a command from God to treat each other the same way that we would treat Jesus Himself.

Not too long ago, I was scheduled to open the business where I work, and shortly after I entered, I heard the phone ringing repeatedly. Usually I do not pick up the phone in the morning until it is almost time to open for business, but on that day, the Lord had different plans. The phone rang and rang, and this person called several times in less than five minutes. Because I did not want to be annoyed by the phone ringing, I decided to pick it up and answer the call.

When I answered, there was a woman on the line who seemed to be crying. Desperately she said, "Please help me. I was there at your store last night for about two hours, and I lost an envelope with my rent money. I've called the police department to ask for help, and I've retraced my last five hours of last night, trying to figure out where I might have lost the envelope. I'm about to be evicted from my apartment if I don't make that payment today."

I felt compassion for the woman, and I told her to call me back in an hour, after I'd had time to see if anyone had found it. In my spirit, I was praying that no one had found it, because I know that most people who find money are not willing to return it to the owner. Before I started my nearly hopeless search, I decided to move a shopping cart that was near the main entrance of the building. As I approached the cart, I noticed that there was a white envelope inside it.

At first, I could not believe that the Lord would answer my prayer so quickly—and that He had blinded so many people from seeing this money until the following day when I would find it. Further exploration revealed that this was indeed the envelope being sought.

I immediately brought the envelope to the office and waited until the woman called back. At 10:04 a.m., only four minutes after we had opened, the woman came in and identified herself as the one who had called about the envelope with the lost money.

I asked her to come with me to the office, and I explained to her what had happened. She wept for joy and thanked God for His mercy toward her. She wanted to hug and kiss me out of appreciation for my honesty. I explained to her that as a Christian, I had just done the right thing, for that was what was expected of me. She went home very happy that the money had been found, praising God that He had sent one of His servants to find the envelope.

I believe that it is our responsibility to act according to our beliefs. The apostle John says that being righteous means doing the right thing, and we must do the right thing in every situation. We need to put ourselves in other people's shoes when making any decision. People of God must realize that every little thing we do on this earth has eternal consequences. Let us do unto others as we want others to do to us.

Choose This Day to Listen

"Then the word of the Lord came to Jonah a second time: 'Go to the great city of Nineveh and proclaim to it the message I give you'" (Jonah 3:2 NIV).

I remember a day when I went home from work a little earlier than usual, as it was a very slow day for business. As soon as I started my car, I began to listen to the book of Jonah on my audio Bible CD. Of the many stories in the Bible, the story of Jonah is one that holds my fascination.

I will summarize the story of Jonah for those who may not know it. The Bible says that God sent Jonah to preach to the city of Nineveh. He was supposed to tell the citizens that they must repent from their sins or they and the whole city would be destroyed by fire. Jonah refused to go, and instead he went on a ship headed to a place far from where God had sent him. In the middle of the sea, a big storm was about to sink the ship, until Jonah was thrown overboard at a spot where God had prepared a big fish to swallow him. Three days later, the fish vomited Jonah onto the coast of Nineveh.

Sometimes this is the case with Christians. God sends us to certain places to do His work, but we decide against going where we've been sent, and we go the opposite direction instead.

Since I lived an hour and twenty minutes away from work, I had the chance to listen to the whole book of Jonah. As I neared my house, the Spirit told me that I must go quickly to the gas station located a few minutes away from my home.

I decided not to listen to the voice of God, and I continued to drive toward my house. Minutes later, the Spirit told me once again to go to the gas station. "Why?" I asked. "I don't need any gas or groceries." I didn't understand why the Lord would want to send me there, but I listened to Him, for I wasn't looking to get swallowed by a great fish, which had happened to Jonah.

As soon as I got out of my car, I heard the voice of a lady who was crying because her car had run out of gas, and she had no way of getting home to her family. She was asking other people for help, but no one seemed to care. Immediately, I understood the reason I was there.

I took my wallet out and gave the woman a twenty-dollar bill. She could not believe that she did not have to ask me. I told her that the Lord Jesus had sent me there to bring twenty dollars to her. She started to cry even more and told me that she had been praying for God to send someone to help her.

My brothers and sisters, if we hear the voice of God's Spirit speak, it is in our best interest to listen and not harden our hearts. If God is asking us do something for Him, there is a reason why He is asking us and not someone else. In His request is a purpose that is greater than we are. We may possess a quality needed for His specified mission.

Do as the Lord says. Let us remember that the Lord is faithful and that He demands our faithfulness. Let us go where He sends us, listen when He speaks to us, and do whatever He requests.

11

Last Days

Wake Up

"So then, let us not be like others, who are asleep, but let us be awake and sober. For those who sleep, sleep at night, and those who get drunk, get drunk at night. But since we belong to the day, let us be sober, putting on faith and love as a breastplate, and the hope of salvation as a helmet" (1 Thessalonians 5:6–8 NIV).

On a Sabbath afternoon, I was meditating on the events of the last day and the end of the world as we know it—and specifically on the twenty-fifth chapter of the gospel of Matthew, which tells the parable of the ten virgins. There we find that five of the virgins fell asleep while waiting for the bridegroom, which, in this case, represents the second coming of Jesus. I asked God for wisdom that I might understand this parable, and on that very same night, I had the following dream:

A great throng was shouting, announcing Christ's second coming, and tumult was everywhere. All those wanting to unite with Christ had to first pass over a hill covered by extremely tall trees. We were told that Christ would be meeting us on the other side of this densely covered hill.

As we walked, I began to notice that these very tall trees bore great amounts of large fruit. I looked up once more and closely observed something that left me rather confused. The fruits were not, in fact, fruits; they were people rolled up and sleeping on the trees as though they were dead. I saw many of my own relatives sleeping there, and I wanted to wake them.

I saw white stones on the ground, and an unknown hand gave me a handful of the stones, which I began to throw at the sleeping bodies, hoping to wake them. After I had used up all my stones, my heart was saddened, for all my efforts had been in vain, and I could not wake anyone. One of the people walking with me told me, "Leave them, Juan. At this point, there's nothing that can wake them." I kept shouting and calling for them to wake up, but no one answered my calls. I reached the end of the forest, and all those who were gathered there looked toward heaven. Then my dream ended.

It is quite evident that the vision I saw was concerned with end-time events. The great throng that shouted and called for us to go out onto the hill represents those who will give earth dwellers a final message of warning to prepare for Christ's soon return. The great hill represents the oncoming tribulation that will soon overtake this world in the coming years. The sleeping people represent those who are indifferent to God's calling. As the Lord says, they are focused on buying, selling, marrying, and giving in marriage. The white stones represent the Word of God, which will be used to try to awaken reason in those who are spiritually asleep.

The condition of God's people is described in Matthew 25. In one way or another, we are sleeping spiritually. We are so used to seeing death, crime, rape, and all kinds of immorality that we become insensible to it. We are so used to seeing sin among us that it no longer affects us when someone practices it in our midst. All the warnings given to us by the prophets are coming to pass right in front of our eyes, and yet we continue not to care.

Every time we listen to a preacher talk about these things, and every time we read a book or a Bible passage mentioning these issues, it is a wake-up call from God. We may be sleeping and not even realize it. We are sleeping when earthly things get our attention more than heavenly things. We are asleep when two or three days pass without our praying. We are asleep when we would rather be in a disco than in church. But we are awake when we see and feel the Spirit of God everywhere we go, in everything we do, and in every thought we have.

It is time for us to wake up and follow the advice from Paul, the apostle: "So then, let us not be like others, who are asleep, but let us be awake and sober. For those who sleep, sleep at night, and those who get drunk, get drunk at night. But since we belong to the day, let us be sober, putting on faith and love as a breastplate, and the hope of salvation as a helmet" (1 Thessalonians 5:6–8 NIV).

Living for Christ

"They will put you out of the synagogue; in fact, the time is coming when anyone who kills you will think they are offering a service to God" (John 6:2 NIV).

Looking through history, we can find many men and women who were willing to die for the name of Christ. Many considered it an honor to suffer for His name. However, even though God wants us to be able to put down our lives for Him if necessary, He wants us to live for Him each day of our lives.

Recently, as I was getting ready to go to bed, I prayed to God and asked Him to remember me when He comes in His glory. I know that the time of the last days will be difficult, unlike any other time witnessed in the history of humanity, as described in the Bible. Therefore, I prayed like I had never prayed before. As I went to sleep, the Lord showed me the following in a dream:

I saw myself working in a place where heavy tools were used. It was a construction site. With me were a few others who had decided to be followers of Jesus. I remember being mocked by all the coworkers who did not profess our same faith. As we worked, we listened to a news station on the radio, and we all heard a news report that panicked those of us who were followers of Christ. The news anchor said, "The government has decreed that any citizen of the United States will be rewarded for killing anyone who professes to follow Jesus, because we know that they don't. If you kill one of them, you are entitled to keep all of their possessions."

Immediately after the news was released, I saw many of my nonbelieving coworkers approaching me and the other believers. Using tools that they were holding in their hands, they began to hit me over the head until I lost consciousness. I remember seeing my body and the bodies of some other believers lying lifeless on the floor. I also saw that our bodies were put together in a big coffin and buried. Though some people cried, many more laughed and felt happy that we had been put to death.

I recall that while their laughter was still on their lips, a big earthquake shook the whole planet. I saw people running in fear from place to place. I saw the ground opening up, and big holes on the earth were swallowing buildings, homes, trees, and seas.

I saw our coffin rise from the grave where it had been placed, the door having opened on its own, and all of those inside opened their eyes. As soon as this took place, I started to see things through the eyes of one who was in the coffin. I screamed with joy and happiness. I knew for sure what was happening. "The Lord has come!" we shouted. "The Lord has come!"

To some people, this may sound like a sci-fi movie, but I believe—I know in my heart of hearts—that this will be the scenario at the end described by John. Many of those who profess to follow Christ will be put to death, but Jesus said, "I am the resurrection, and the life: he that believeth on me, though he die, yet shall he live" (John 6:12 ASV).

God is not demanding that we die for Him. Rather, the Lord is asking that we *live* for Him, that we make it our will to do His work and finish it. He desires that we live our lives on earth in anticipation of the life that is to come when He makes all things new.

The Antichrist

"Let no one deceive you in any way. For that day will not come, unless the rebellion comes first, and the man of lawlessness is revealed, the son of destruction" (2 Thessalonians 2:3 ESV).

On one occasion, as I studied 2 Thessalonians 2, I could not understand what the apostle Paul was revealing in this account. I wanted to know its meaning, since I believe that it is connected to the final chapter of the history of humankind. So I asked the Lord in prayer to open my understanding, grant my mind clarity, and reveal the contents of 2 Thessalonians 2:8–10: "Then that lawless one will be revealed whom the Lord will slay with the breath of His mouth and bring to an end by the appearance of His coming; that is, the one whose coming is in accord with the activity of Satan, with all power and signs and false wonders, and with all the deception of wickedness for those who perish, because they did not receive the love of the truth so as to be saved."

That same night when I went to sleep, the Lord showed me His revelation in the form of a dream:

I was with a group of friends and brothers in the faith, and together we were preaching the word of God in New York City. My brothers and sisters preached the gospel powerfully, warning the world of Christ's imminent second coming. Many believed, but many more refused to repent and leave their lives of sin behind them.

Suddenly we heard a loud sound of horns and trumpets playing in unison. A great ship of gigantic proportions covered the sky, and it was followed by thousands upon thousands of smaller ships. These ships were like none ever witnessed by any man. They had a rectangular aspect and a light in their midst that was so bright that it was visible even in the noon light. The mother ship landed on the earth, while all the smaller ships remained hovering in the air. All present were waiting in anticipation to see what would take place next.

Suddenly the great door on the ship opened to reveal a figure resembling a man. He stood in the doorway and then walked forth to the outside. As he exited, he played a great trumpet that shook the entire city, and a great earthquake caused a great deal of damage. Many who were with me proclaimed with a loud voice, "It is the Lord Jesus Christ!," and a great majority of those who had not yet accepted the message of salvation rejoiced and went to meet this person.

This semblance of a man was like the description of Jesus in Revelation 3. He had hair flowing to his shoulders, and his face shone, reflecting glory and power that had never been witnessed by any human being. I saw that all religious and political leaders united to greet their lord. The pope prepared to grant him Saint Peter's throne in the Vatican, and all the world rejoiced at this man's coming.

A smaller group of people began to warn all those who were rejoicing over this man's return, saying that this was not the Jesus spoken of in the Bible but was rather a wolf in sheep's clothing—the Devil himself. I was present as well, shouting unceasingly that same warning with my brothers and sisters. Moments later, I heard this false Christ say that the small group who refused to believe in him was dividing all of humanity and that doing so warranted their deaths. I remember that we were all persecuted, and many of us were captured or killed for unmasking this false Christ.

Upon waking, I quickly wrote a summary of what I had just dreamed, thanking the Lord for giving me clarity once again in understanding the text. I firmly believe with all my heart that Satan will one day reenact and personify Jesus's second coming so vividly that he will lead astray the majority of the selected few. In fact, Jesus Himself warned His followers, "Then if anyone tells you, 'Look, here is the Messiah,' or 'There he is,' don't believe it" (Mark 13:21 NIV).

The Scriptures clearly teach us that Christ's second coming is to be a global event. Every human eye will see Him descending in the clouds. In that very moment, the dead in Christ shall rise, being transformed into the image of Christ. "For the Lord Himself will descend from heaven with a shout, with the voice of the archangel and with the trumpet of God, and the dead in Christ will rise first. Then we who are alive and remain will be caught up together with them in the clouds to meet the Lord in the air, and so we shall always be with the Lord" (1 Thessalonians 4:16–17 KJV).

Juan D. Bautista

It is not my intention to say that I have received the final revelation or interpretation of these verses. However, I believe that it is extremely important for us to understand their meaning. There are millions of men and women who have sincere hearts and love the Lord with all their might. I also believe that the man of sin who pretends to be God will soon be revealed to us as described in the Bible verses above. It is our duty to study the Word of God diligently, asking the Spirit of Jesus to enlighten us as we learn these amazing truths.

12

Faith

Dying before Denying

"Do not be afraid of those who kill the body but cannot kill the soul. Rather, be afraid of the One who can destroy both soul and body in hell" (Matthew 10:28 NIV).

Though I want to express my own personal experiences to demonstrate God's supernatural power and greatness, I think God uses the experiences of others to strengthen my own faith. Some years ago, while attending a church service in New York City, I heard an amazing story of a pastor living in the Soviet Union in the early 1920s. In those early years, many nations still persecuted those who professed faith in Jesus Christ, and this pastor was imprisoned for not denying his faith or his God.

Two days after his imprisonment, the prison's warden came into the pastor's cell and asked, "Do you want to go free? Deny your God!" The pastor replied, "No, I would die before denying my God." The warden turned away and left. The next day, the warden returned and asked the same question, and the pastor repeated his answer. This routine went on for two weeks, after which the warden decided to change his tactics.

He came in after those two weeks and said, "We will see if you won't deny your God. Starting today, you will no longer receive food—until the day you finally decide to deny your God and your faith." The first day passed, and the pastor was not given any food. The second day passed, and then the third day also, and still the pastor received no food. The pastor began to weaken, but he prayed to God for mercy.

The warden returned on the fourth day and asked, "Are you ready to deny your God?" With a weakened voice, the pastor replied, "Never." When the warden left, the pastor began to pray, "My Lord, for Your name's sake, let me not die in this manner. Show these people that You are indeed God. Show them why my faith and trust are placed in You."

When the pastor finished praying, he saw a cat approaching his cell with a loaf of bread in its mouth, which it dropped by the pastor's feet. Three times a day, for the next two days, the cat brought him bread, and the pastor praised God for His love and grace. Three days after the cat had begun to feed the pastor, the warden decided to visit his prisoner's cell, hoping to find a dead man or a man ready to deny his God and his faith.

To the warden's surprise, he found a man standing on his feet, singing praises to God. "Are you ready to deny your God?" the warden asked.

The pastor answered, "Never!"

"Then you will die from hunger in this cell," said the warden.

The pastor looked at him and said, "My God has been bringing me food three times a day."

"What? Who? How?" asked the warden. "I want to know who has been feeding you so that I may execute him this instant for disobeying my orders." While the warden was still talking, the cat walked in carrying a loaf of bread, and the warden began to cry. "My God! This is my cat, and the bread he brings is from my table, which has been disappearing over the last few days."

After this experience, the warden and all his family believed in God's almighty power, gave their lives to Christ, and were baptized.

Praise be to God, who makes impossible things look easy. I was changed greatly by this man's testimony. My faith and my spiritual life were strengthened. God uses anything and everything in our favor. The pastor was saved by his perseverance, the warden and his family were saved by God's revealed power, and I myself have been saved by being born again in Christ Jesus after hearing the amazing testimonies of people such as this pastor.

Let everything that has breath praise the Lord!

13

Conclusion

It is my hope that the reader's spiritual strength may be renewed by reading the personal experiences expressed in each of the stories told in this book. May the dreams and visions revealed here open our eyes to a new light. May we see that this world is soon to pass and that God is calling His people to "flee from Babylon!"

May God's message illuminate our hearts and strengthen our faith enough to move and shake mountains. May we realize that we are living in the last days, and may we decide to prepare ourselves for Jesus's imminent and triumphant return, that He may find a people faithfully awaiting Him.

Jesus is coming soon. The mere sound of these words should produce feelings of both joy and fear in the hearts of men. We should feel *joy*, because all the pain, suffering, evil acts of violence, and death will finally come to an end. We should feel *fear*, because the words should cause us to search our hearts and minds and ask ourselves, "Am I truly ready to withstand that day?" Can we—those of us who claim to believe—honestly say that we are ready to encounter Jesus at His second advent? Do our lives reflect the faith that we profess, and does our faith produce works to complement it?

What are we doing with our lives to prepare for the soon second coming of Christ? This is a question that should permeate the thinking of all of Christ's followers. We must consider all that we claim to believe, and ask ourselves, "What is it all for? Aren't my beliefs meant to shape my life, to prepare it for the heavenly kingdom? If so, then I should act according to my beliefs, and not simply state that I believe."

Our brother James states in his book, "Show me your faith without your works, and I will show you my faith by my works" (James 2:18 NKJV).

He was trying to teach us that faith cannot exist without works. Without works, the faith we proclaim is a dead faith—mere words spoken to sound important in front of others.

It is time for us as believers to take a stand for what we believe. The world is quickly working to turn its back on God, denying Him credit for the creation He has made. A time is coming soon and is nearly upon us, when the world will unite to persecute those who uphold Christ's teachings and God's commandments as the ultimate law for mankind. On which side will we find ourselves?

God is sending His workers to warn the world of the chaos approaching the earth, and He seeks to save all those who are willing to be saved. In the words of Joshua, "If it is disagreeable in your sight to serve the Lord, choose for yourselves today whom you will serve: whether the gods which your fathers served which were beyond the River, or the gods of the Amorites in whose land you are living; but as for me and my house, we will serve the Lord" (Joshua 24:15 NIV).

It is the individual's decision to believe—or not to believe—in the power of God. The Lord is real and good. He is marvelous in all His works. Praise His name, all you inhabitants of the earth. Everything that is alive, praise His name and glorify Him who made heaven and earth!

About the Author

Juan D. Bautista is a Christian evangelist who travels throughout the United States preaching the word of God. Teaching is his greatest passion and sharing the gospel is his life's mission. He lives with his wife and three children in Connecticut.